WARW

GHOST STORIES

Compiled by Julia Skinner

THE FRANCIS FRITH COLLECTION

www.francisfrith.com

First published in the United Kingdom in 2013 by The Francis Frith Collection®

This edition published exclusively for Bradwell Books in 2013
For trade enquiries see: www.bradwellbooks.com or tel: 0800 834 920
ISBN 978-1-84589-743-7

British Library Cataloguing in Publication Data

Haunted Warwickshire - Ghost Stories
Compiled by Julia Skinner

The Francis Frith Collection
6 Oakley Business Park,
Wylye Road, Dinton,
Wiltshire SP3 5EU
Tel: +44 (0) 1722 716 376
Email: info@francisfrith.co.uk
www.francisfrith.com

Printed and bound in Malaysia
Contains material sourced from responsibly managed forests

Front Cover: **WARWICK, THE CASTLE, CAESAR'S TOWER AND GUY'S TOWER 1922**
72366p
Frontispiece: **KENILWORTH, THE CASTLE FROM THE BRIDGE c1870** K530I

The colour-tinting is for illustrative purposes only, and is not intended to be historically accurate

CONTENTS

HAUNTED WARWICKSHIRE

One of Warwickshire's saddest ghost stories comes from Little Compton in the extreme south of the county, near the Oxfordshire border. The tale goes that back in the 1870s the curate of its parish church of St Denys fell desperately in love with a beautiful young lady who sang in the church choir. Unfortunately she did not share his feelings, and had ambitions for a better match for herself than a lowly curate. Instead, she accepted the offer of another suitor of higher social standing and wealthier means, and the curate had to conduct their marriage ceremony. When the wedding service was over he claimed a kiss from the bride, then made his way to the belfry of the church where he hanged himself in despair. His heartbroken shade has haunted the building and the churchyard ever since.

North-east of Little Compton is Long Compton, which in the past was famous for the number of witches who lived in the area. The witches were said to meet at the Close Field on Harrow Hill, which has been associated with witchcraft, black magic and paranormal activity for centuries, perhaps because of its proximity to the Rollright Stones, a mysterious complex of Neolithic and Bronze Age megalithic monuments. The area is supposed to be haunted by a ghostly old hag with dirty matted hair, reputedly the ghost of Anne Tennant, an old woman of Romany origin who was attacked with a pitchfork in the 1870s by a drunken neighbour, James Heywood, and died of her wounds. James Heywood claimed she had bewitched him, and declared when he was arrested that 'there are 16 other witches in the same area who deserve the same fate'. He was deemed to be insane and locked away in Warwick jail, where he died a few months later. Witnesses who have seen the wraith of 'old Annie' describe her as a hideous old crone, dressed in ragged clothing and a black shawl, who mysteriously appears around the village and vanishes away if you approach her. Harrow Hill itself is also said to be haunted by a spectral coach-and-four which travels around the area on a never-ending ghostly journey.

Another phantom coach is associated with Ilmington, near Shipston on Stour, which is haunted by a ghostly carriage drawn by six headless black horses, particularly around Pig Lane, an ancient route that is now a bridle path. One tale says it carries the ghost of a local landowner who killed one of his neighbours, whilst another says it is a one-wheeled coach that carries the ghost of a murdered man – despite its limited wheel-power, it manages to travel a spectral route around the village, leaving the track of its single wheel in the ground to betray its passing. Be sure not to go looking for the carriage on Christmas Eve or New Year's Eve though, as on those nights the area between Ilmington and Meon Hill to the west is supposed to be roamed by a phantom huntsman and his pack of hounds. One tradition about him is that he was a 17th-century squire of Ilmington Manor who loved hunting so much that he rode out on the chase even on Sundays, neglecting his church attendance; eventually he received his come-uppance for not giving the Sabbath day its due reverence, when a chasm opened in the ground and swallowed him up, together with his hounds, and none of them were ever seen again in earthly form. If you ever meet the huntsman, take care not to do anything that he asks, for this gives him the power to carry you away with him and share his doom of eternal damnation.

In Ilmington itself, the church of St Mary is reputed to be haunted by the ghost of Edward Golding, a former rector who died in 1793. His memorial in the church bears the intriguing inscription that 'His performance of the duties of his office fell far short of their obligations and importance; but rests in the Hope of Mercy through the Saviour' – but despite that hope, unfortunately his spirit does not seem to be resting easy and a number of witnesses over the years have reported seeing his apparition walking about the church. One lady described how it walked towards her whilst she was arranging flowers on the altar and then just faded away, 'as if one was turning off a television programme'.

On the corner of New Street and West Street in Shipston on Stour in south Warwickshire is the Old Council House, an imposing building that was originally a rectory; in the 20th century it housed offices for Shipston Rural Council, and subsequently Stratford District Council, but it is now residential once again. According to the town's Heritage Walks leaflet, the building is reputed to be haunted by a ghostly old lady dressed in black.

North of Shipston on Stour is Tredington, where the parish church of St Gregory has the tallest spire in Warwickshire. For many years there was a local tale that the cheerful shade of an old lady called Betty used to sit on the churchyard wall beside the road, smoking her pipe and nodding her head in friendly greeting to passers-by. Apparently Betty was a white witch who lived in the village in the 18th century, skilled in the collection of herbs, berries and beneficial plants and making natural remedies for the local people. A kind and helpful old lady in her earthly life, after her death her friendly shade continued to roam the area where she had lived and worked.

North of Tredington is Halford, where a mysterious elderly lady wearing old-fashioned clothing and a traditional white sun-bonnet sometimes appears at dusk, walking along the road carrying a basket – just like the lady photographed in 1910 at Broom, near Bidford-on-Avon, on the opposite page. Witnesses who have seen her have reported that she walks straight towards them – and then just vanishes away before their eyes…

Further north up the A3400, the stretch of road near the entrance to Alscot Park is roamed by the ghost of a farmer who died whilst riding home at night, after taking a wager on the time it would take to ride his horse between Alderminster and Atherstone on Stour in the dark. As he galloped along, he failed to notice a bough of a tree overhanging his route – he hit it at breakneck speed, and was unseated from his horse and killed. The local legend is that if you see his wraith, you are bound to see it again on two more occasions.

A famous haunted location in Warwickshire is what is now the luxurious Ettington Park Hotel, previously known as Ettington Hall, off the A3400 near Alderminster south of Stratford-upon-Avon. Ettington Hall was the home of the Shirley family for centuries, and the mansion has been much altered and extended over the years. Its present incarnation is the result of a major rebuilding programme in the mid 19th century to designs of the architect John Prichard. Its neo-Gothic architecture gives this imposing Victorian mansion the appearance of a typical haunted house of popular imagination – so much so that it was used for the exterior shots of the haunted house in the classic 1963 horror film 'The Haunting'. Despite its reputation as one of the most haunted hotels in Britain, Ettington Park's ghosts are said to be harmless and don't disturb its visitors with any threatening or malevolent activity. However, if ghost hunting is your thing, here are some of the spectral residents you might encounter on a visit there:

Strange incidents in the area around the entrance door and the reception desk include a lighted candle 'floating' above the oak mantelpiece, and the shadowy form of a man crossing the reception area accompanied by his equally shadowy dog, and disappearing into the Library. That room is also the scene of strange phenomena, including a noticeable cold spot to the right-hand side of the fireplace and poltergeist-type activity in the form of a book falling from its shelf with some force, as if being thrown by an unseen hand – uncannily, it is always the same book, 'St Ronan's Well' by Sir Walter Scott. The sound of men talking has also been heard emanating from the Library when no one is there, accompanied by what seems to be the clink of billiard balls in a ghostly re-enactment of a game of billiards played there at some time in the past. Disembodied voices, particularly of women, have also been heard in the Great Drawing Room, where a barefooted lady in Edwardian costume has also been seen standing by the bay window on the right hand side of the room; doors and curtains have also been mysteriously opened and closed in this room, apparently by an invisible hand.

A particularly atmospheric part of Ettington is the Long Gallery, where some people have experienced a very strong feeling of being watched by something unseen, and others have reported seeing a mysterious elderly lady standing by the last bay window next to the fireplace. A ghostly man who appears to be an army officer is also said to linger in this part of the hotel.

One of the best-known spirit residents of Ettington is believed to be the ghost of a servant girl who died after falling down the main staircase, pushed to her death during a violent argument with someone. She has been seen on and near the staircase, and also haunts the Oak Room, a part of the mansion where dogs sometimes seem distressed, as if sensing the presence of something unseen. A spectral elderly lady in Victorian dress haunts the Conservatory, where disembodied footsteps walking back and forth across the empty room have also been heard, and the wraith of a woman wearing a long white gown, who has become known as 'Lady Emma', is said to roam both the Tower Suite corridor and the Stour corridor, possibly the shade of a governess who worked at the house in the past. In 1975 a member of staff at Ettington also saw 'Lady Emma' gliding along the hallway and walking along the cloister-like terrace beside the arched entrance before disappearing into a wall 'as if she melted into it'.

The ghosts of two young children, thought to have drowned in the River Stour where it flows through the Ettington estate in the early 19th century, have also been seen and heard as they run and play around the house as well as in its grounds, where frequent sightings of a ghostly monk have also been reported.

For more information about the paranormal activity linked with this fascinating place, see 'A Brief Guide to the Ghosts at Ettington Park' on the History section of the hotel's website: www.handpickedhotels.co.uk/hotels/ettington-park-hotel

South Warwickshire was the location of the first pitched battle of the English Civil War of the 17th century, between the Parliamentarian forces led by the Earl of Essex and the Royalist forces led by King Charles I and his nephew Prince Rupert. Known to history as the battle of Edgehill, this was fought on 23rd October 1642 on land below the escarpment of Edge Hill, between the villages of Kineton and Radway. The battle ended indecisively, and both sides claimed victory. Ghostly re-enactments of the battle are said to have taken place around the battlefield site on many occasions ever since. The first report was by two shepherds, who told how on the night of 23rd/24th December in 1642, the year of the battle, they heard the sound of men fighting, the sound of drums and trumpets and the roar of cannonfire, accompanied by the sight of phantom soldiers fighting in the sky – although terrified, the shepherds stayed through the night to watch the phantom armies re-enacting the battle until dawn broke. They told a local magistrate and a parson about the ghostly battle, and those two men went to the battlefield the following night and saw the same spectral conflict. On hearing of the ghostly goings on, Charles I sent a party to investigate. They returned and told the king that they themselves had seen the ghostly battle re-fought and had even been able to identify a number of the people taking part, who had been killed in the real battle. In January 1643 a pamphlet was published titled 'Apparitions and Prodigious Noyses of War and Battels seen on Edge Hill near Keinton in Warwickshire'. This was the first documented account of many ghostly re-enactments of the battle that have been witnessed on countless occasions over the centuries, on both 23rd October, the anniversary of the battle, and on the night of 23rd/24th December. The visual manifestation of the ghostly armies has not been seen for some years now, but the sounds of the battle are still said to echo back from the past, most frequently on the October date. A mysterious phantom horse-rider on his white steed has also been seen on the battlefield site.

In the 1740s Sanderson Miller, a local squire, began to build an octagonal folly at the village of Edge Hill to mark the spot where the Royal Standard was raised and to commemorate the 100th anniversary of the battle of Edgehill; the building was formally opened on 3rd September 1750, the anniversary of the death of Oliver Cromwell. It is suitably warlike in character, for it does indeed look like a well-fortified castle – the main tower was loosely modelled on Guy's Tower at Warwick Castle. The building was originally known as Radway Castle or Radway Tower, but it became the Castle Inn during Queen Victoria's reign. The inn is perched on the summit of Edge Hill, and from its garden there is a wonderful view of the battlefield site down below. Inside the inn is a collection of weapons found on the battlefield, and even a resident ghost – a spectral soldier from the battle is said to ride through the bar!

EDGE HILL, THE CASTLE INN 1922 72072

A sad ghost linked with the Civil War battle of Edgehill in 1642 roams Lighthorne, a few miles north of the battlefield site, east of Wellesbourne. A young man from the village went off to fight on the side of Parliament against the king, fired up with the righteousness of the cause, but met his death on the battlefield. He had married just a few months earlier, and his heartbroken young wife pined away and died of grief soon afterwards. Her weeping shade is said to roam Church Lane in the village, still mourning her lost love.

Off the B4088 between Wellesbourne and Stratford-upon-Avon is Charlecote Park, which was owned by the Lucy family from c1200 until 1945 when the property passed to the National Trust. The present house was begun in the mid 16th century by Sir Thomas Lucy, but has been much altered since then. Charlecote is now displayed to the public as it would have been in the 19th century with its interior preserved as an excellent study in Victorian taste. Charlecote's service wing is also open to the public, containing the scullery, kitchen, laundry and brewhouse, as well as the stables, coach house and tack-room. In his book 'This Haunted Isle' of 1984, Peter Underwood recorded an interview with Lady Fairfax-Lucy in which she described paranormal activity that had been experienced in the Green Room of Charlecote Park, a bedroom in the original part of the old house in the family's private accommodation in the west wing. The Green Room used to have a door opening on to the Minstrels' Gallery above the Great Hall, which was taken down in the 1870s, and still has a small room leading off it which would have been used by the musicians in the past. Lady Fairfax-Lucy recounted how several family members, including herself, had heard 'an unidentifiable hubbub' of raised voices coming from that small room, which sounded as if some sort of ghostly argument was taking place there, 'accompanied by violent actions'.

The lake in the grounds of Charlecote Park is reputed to be haunted by the spectre of a tragic young woman, possibly a servant of the house at some time in the past, who drowned herself there, for reasons now unknown. In a ghostly re-enactment of her suicide, her shadowy figure glides down from the house to the lake, throws herself into the water and then mysteriously disappears beneath its surface – but there is never any sound of a splash, nor any ripples on the water…

CHARLECOTE, THE PARK c1955 C251001

STRATFORD-UPON-AVON, HENLEY STREET, SHAKESPEARE'S BIRTHPLACE AFTER RESTORATION 1861 S21602

Stratford-upon-Avon is famous for its connection with William Shakespeare, who was born in April 1564 in a house in Henley Street and grew up there; it was also where he lived with his wife Anne Hathaway for the first five years of their marriage and where their three children were born. The house is now open to the public and run as a museum to the great poet and playwright. In her book 'Haunted Warwickshire' of 1981, Meg Elizabeth Atkins records that for some time in the 1940s the property was haunted by a kindly old lady with white hair and rosy cheeks, wearing an old-fashioned black gown and black cap, who sat working at a spinning wheel in an upstairs room. She appeared so real that many visitors thought she was a member of staff and tried to talk to her; however, as soon as she became aware of their presence she would turn to the onlookers, politely murmur 'Good day, my dears' – and then vanish away before their eyes!

William Shakespeare was lucky to survive his childhood, for in 1564 – the year of his birth – Stratford was afflicted with a terrible outbreak of plague. Amongst those who died was Charlotte Clopton, who lived at Clopton House to the north of the town. The mansion that stands today (now converted into residential apartments) dates from the 17th century, with 19th-century rebuilds and additions, and was constructed around the 16th-century manor house that was the earlier home of the Clopton family. The story goes that after her death Charlotte was buried in the vault of the Clopton chapel attached to Holy Trinity Church at Stratford. Another member of the Clopton family died a few weeks after her death, and when his coffin was taken into the vault, Charlotte's body was found leaning against the wall; it appeared that she had not actually been dead when she was interred, and had woken from a coma to find herself buried alive. She had broken out of her coffin and managed to survive for a while, but eventually died of hunger and despair after trying to claw her way out of the vault. Her ghost is said to have haunted her family home ever since.

Some people believe Shakespeare had Charlotte's terrible fate in mind when he wrote the ending of his tragedy 'Romeo and Juliet', in which Juliet feigns death by taking a drug that puts her into a deathlike coma to escape the marriage arranged by her parents; before swallowing the draught, she imagines the horror of waking in the tomb before (she hopes) Romeo arrives to rescue her: 'Is it not very like the horrible conceit of death and night, together with the terror of the place?'. A story about an earlier member of the family, Margaret Clopton, may also have inspired him when he was writing about Ophelia's suicide in 'Hamlet'. She had fallen in love with a young man but her father disapproved of him and forbade them to marry. In despair at losing her true love, Margaret drowned herself in a well in the grounds of the house. Her sad wraith is said to haunt the spot in the silent watches of the night.

WILLIAM SHAKESPEARE (1564-1616) S216504

In 1597 William Shakespeare purchased a house in Church Street in Stratford-upon-Avon, known as New Place (which, sadly, was demolished in 1759). He retired there at the end of his acting and playwriting career, and it was where he died in 1616. Holy Trinity Church at Stratford is his burial place, where his grave slab famously bears the words:

> *'Good frend for Jesus sake forbeare*
> *To digg the dust encloased heare*
> *Bleste be ye man yt spares thes stones*
> *And curst be he yt moves my bones.'*

Shakespeare's grave has remained undisturbed, as he requested, so his curse has not been activated and his spirit remains at peace. However, many restless spirits are said to roam a building near the church that was once the home of his eldest daughter, Suzanna, and her physician husband, Dr John Hall – Hall's Croft in Old Town. This historic timber-framed house is now open to the public with an exhibition about Dr Hall and a display of Elizabethan surgical equipment. The ghosts reputed to linger in Hall's Croft include a man dressed in Elizabethan-style clothes who has been seen looking down to the street from the first-floor windows, ghostly children whose footsteps have been heard running up and down the stairs, and the spirit of Betty Legett, who lived there in the early decades of the 20th century with her sister and died after falling down the staircase in 1931. Visitors sometimes report feeling a sensation like a gentle push on their backs whilst they are standing on the stairs, but no one knows if this is Betty's spirit trying to make them fall down the stairs like she did, or if, perhaps, she is trying to communicate that she didn't fall by accident, and was actually pushed to her death. In February 2004 Hall's Croft was one of the locations in Stratford visited by the team from television's 'Most Haunted' series, for a two-day live broadcast. The team included the presenter Yvette Fielding and the medium Derek Acorah, who felt the presence of a number of spirits in the house, including Betty's. However, not all the ghostly residents of Hall's Croft seemed pleased about the team being there, as during their investigation a spoon suddenly flew through the air as if flung at Yvette Fielding, and landed on the floor with a loud clatter. The phenomenon was caught on camera as part of the live broadcast, to the astonishment of all who saw it – but was even more uncanny because the spoon that flew was part of the exhibition of objects in the building, and was actually kept wired down to the table on which it lay…

As part of their two-day live television broadcast in February 2004, the 'Most Haunted' paranormal investigation team also visited another famous haunted location in Stratford-upon-Avon that William Shakespeare would have known well, the Shrieve's House and Barn in Sheep Street. In Shakespeare's day the house was a tavern run by William Rogers, whose daughter Elizabeth was a friend of his daughter Suzanna, but this historic building now houses part of one of Stratford's most popular attractions, Tudor World, which tells the story of the town's history and gives a flavour of what life was like in England in Shakespeare's lifetime. (At the time of the 'Most Haunted' investigation the attraction was known as the Falstaff's Experience.)

The Shrieve's House and Barn dates from the 1500s and has stood in the town during fires, outbreaks of plague and the turmoil of the Civil War – wounded soldiers were brought there to be tended after the battle of Edgehill in 1642. Countless scenes of drama, tragedy and sorrow must have occurred under its roof, and there are rumours of sorcery, witchcraft and black magic practices having taken place in the building in the past, which is widely believed to be one of the most haunted places in Britain. Paranormal investigations have suggested that the building is regularly visited by up to 40 ghosts, the most famous of which is the shade of its first known tenant, William Shrieve, who was an archer to King Henry VIII and was in residence from 1536; others include a murderer from the 18th century, a small girl who in her earthly life was a pickpocket in the building when it was a tavern and now amuses herself by moving the exhibits around at night, and what the attraction's website describes as 'a dark hooded figure with red glowing eyes, said to be a very ancient spirit' that materialises at certain times of year.

When the 'Most Haunted' team visited the Shrieve's House and Barn for their investigation in 2004, the film crew initially experienced strange losses of power with their electrical equipment which caused their lights to keep fading, forcing the team members to conduct their investigation by torchlight. As they wandered around in the darkness they felt themselves pelted with small objects, and later found a number of small stones on the floor. Then, live on camera, Derek Acorah appeared to be possessed by some sort of malevolent entity as he made his way upstairs, which he later described in a letter to the Shrieve's House staff as 'a particularly bad soul, trying desperately to unnerve me'; he wrote that it was one of the most frightening experiences he had ever encountered. The full text of Derek Acorah's letter can be read on the Tudor World website www.falstaffexperience.co.uk using the link for 'Ghosts' and then 'Paranormal Investigation Groups'.

There have been far more reports of ghosts and paranormal activity in the Shrieve's House and Barn than there is room to record here, but there is more detailed information on its website, which also features a gallery of intriguing photographs that have been taken by visitors around the property. These views seem to show light orbs, unexplained misty shapes, strange streaks of light and curious thermal images, as well as several mysterious shadowy figures – to see them, go to the Tudor World website www.falstaffexperience. co.uk and follow the link for 'Ghosts' and then 'Ghostly Pictures'.

If you've got strong nerves you can also go on a guided ghost walk around this fascinating building, but be warned – many visitors who have done so have reported feeling dizzy or nauseous, or been overwhelmed by a sense of depression. Others have experienced feelings of being pushed, pulled, stroked or pinched by unseen hands, and two people who spent the night watching for ghosts in the Shrieve's House in 2004 described it as the most terrifying night of their lives…

This photograph shows the 16th-century Falcon Inn at Bidford-on-Avon, a few miles west of Stratford, as it appeared in 1901 – it is no longer a pub, and the building has now been converted into private homes. The Falcon Inn is reputed to have been the scene of a drinking competition between the young William Shakespeare and his friends and a group of local lads known as the Bidford Sippers. The Stratford boys lost the bout and were too drunk to make the journey home, so they spent the night sleeping off the session under a crab-apple tree. When morning dawned, Shakespeare's friends wished to renew the encounter. However, he declined to join in and is supposed to have replied with a piece of doggerel about various places in the area, saying he had supped with lads from 'Piping Pebworth, Dancing Marston, Haunted Hillborough, Hungry Grafton, Dodging Exhall, Papist Wixford, Beggarly Broom and Drunken Bidford', and had therefore had enough.

BIDFORD-ON-AVON, THE OLD FALCON INN 1901 47340

The 'Haunted Hillborough' of the rhyme refers to the tiny hamlet of Hillborough which is south of the B439 between Bidford-on-Avon and Stratford, showing that even in Shakespeare's day this area had a reputation for its ghosts. The 16th-century manor house at Hillborough is supposed to be roamed by a mysterious White Lady, who may be the same spectre that wanders the area accompanied by a white stag; she has been described variously as a nun, the shade of Anne Whateley, a daughter of the house in Shakespeare's time, and an elderly lady. A phantom carriage and pair drives around Hillborough Lane, and the ghost of a man called Palmer who was found guilty of murdering his wife haunts the spot where in 1801 he was hanged and his body was left to rot on the gibbet; in fact, his wraith was so active there in the past that the field where the gibbet had stood became known as Palmer's Piece.

A short distance further north, the A46 runs between Stratford-upon-Avon and Alcester, passing the picturesque Stag Inn where it stands beside the road at Redhill. Parts of this historic building date from the 16th century, and in the 17th century the Stag was being used as the local court, with a small prison cell, as well as an inn. A fascinating relic of that time still survives in the inn, where the old door to the prison cell can still be seen, strengthened with iron studs to make it more secure. The mysterious ghost of an elderly woman dressed in old-fashioned dark clothes is said to haunt the inn, who may be the sad shade of a woman whose son was tried at the old court at the Stag for highway robbery many years ago; after being sentenced to death he was hanged from an oak tree near a crossroads not far from the inn, and his mother died of grief a few days later.

ALCESTER, THE OLD TOWN HALL c1965 A113043

The lower storey of Alcester's picturesque old Town Hall was the first part to be built, in 1618, as an open market place for traders. The upper room was added in 1641, with an impressive hammerbeam roof. The ground floor was enclosed in the 19th century and used as a local court, and a basement prison known as 'The Hole', which is still there, served as the town's lock-up until 1850. A number of restless spirits are reputed to haunt this historic building, which include a mysterious Grey Lady and the unhappy shade of a young girl that roams the upper storey and can be heard crying. The sound of disembodied footsteps has also been heard in the main hall, and the witness who heard them recounted that when he went to see who was there, the footsteps continued to pace across the floor even though no one else was in the room; he was also aware that the temperature in the room was noticeably cold, and described what seemed to be a wispy cloud of mist or fog that hovered high up in the hall, near the roof…

The old Town Hall is one of several places in Alcester that are supposed to be haunted by the wraith of Captain Richard Hill, an unsavoury character who in 1693 came to lodge at what was then the Angel Inn in Church Street, very near the Town Hall; it has now been converted into two residential dwellings. His good looks and genial manner initially charmed the town's high society, but he was actually a murderer and rapist who was on the run, and his true nature showed itself when he was invited to a party at the Pumphrey family home (now Churchill House). He got into a violent argument during a card game, drew his sword and attacked his fellow players. He was thrown out of the house and went back to the inn threatening vengeance against the company he had just left. A short time later he disappeared, and the story was put about that he had left town. However, it was widely suspected that he had been murdered at the Angel by those he had threatened, and it was around that time that tales of the inn being haunted first began. Many, many years later, during renovations after the inn had become a private house, a large oven was discovered bricked up behind a wall in the sitting room; inside the oven was a wooden box containing some of Captain Hill's clothes and belongings, including his two swords, which he would have been unlikely to leave behind if he had left the inn voluntarily. Was he killed at the inn and his remains disposed of in some macabre fashion? It would appear so, as the haunting of the old Angel building intensified after the box was discovered. Most witness reports tell of a 'phosphorescent man' appearing in the bedrooms, who rattled doors and drawer handles and rocked the furniture, but in one account the wraith is described as a shimmering misty shape that glided along the room until it faded away into the shadows – could that possibly be the same entity as the wispy cloud of mist that has been seen in the upper room of the old Town Hall?

Just south of Alcester is Ragley Hall, a magnificent Palladian mansion that is the ancestral seat of the Marquess of Hertford. A long-held local tradition is that a spot near the gates of Ragley's park is haunted by a White Lady who sometimes appears there at midnight, sitting on a fence or stile, before moving to a nearby spring where her shadowy figure bends down to drink the water. Perhaps she is the shade of the Anglo-Saxon lady from many centuries ago who was buried near the spring after her death; her skeleton was discovered there in 1833, together with some jewellery and a small dagger. Another White Lady who is said to roam around Ragley's park dressed in a long white gown is identified in local legend as the wraith of an Italian girl employed as a maid at the hall in the 18th century. She is supposed to have been murdered in a jealous rage by her lover, who also worked at the hall, who hid her body in the grounds before fleeing away.

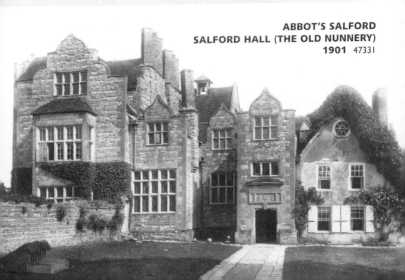

ABBOT'S SALFORD
SALFORD HALL (THE OLD NUNNERY)
1901 47331

About six miles south of Alcester is Abbot's Salford. Originally Salteford Minor, the village was re-named Abbot's Salford after a 15th-century Abbot of Evesham built a timber-framed country house there as a guest residence for the monks; part of that original house survives as the west wing of what is now the Salford Hall Hotel, the rest of which dates mostly from c1600 when the building became a family residence after the Reformation. Salford Hall was occupied by a community of Benedictine nuns between 1807 and 1838, and it is still sometimes called the Old Nunnery.

If you are looking for a paranormal dimension to an away-break, the Salford Hall Hotel might be a good place to visit – the building is said to be rife with paranormal activity and is often on the itinerary of ghost hunting tours. If you are lucky, the ethereal shades of a nun, several monks and a group of young girls are among the spirits you might encounter. The spectral nun is the ghost most commonly seen, usually on the lower floor of the building; the local tale is that in her earthly life she was murdered in the house in the 17th century, and has wandered the building ever since. You might see the phantom monks striding through the hotel in an echo of their visit there hundreds of years ago, but you'll only see them for a few moments before they vanish away before your eyes; and watch out for the two priests that some people have seen walking through the courtyard, more visitors from the past who have yet to leave the building. Some of the hotel's spectral residents are not seen at all, but only heard – listen very carefully in the reception area and you might hear the sound of that group of young girls giggling at some joke from the past. The hotel's ghosts are not threatening, but many people have reported a strong sense of being watched intently by unseen eyes – it seems that Salford Hall's spectral residents are just as interested in you as you are in them…

North of Alcester just off the A435 is Coughton Court, a grand mansion that has been the home of the Throckmorton family since 1409, although the family now manages the Coughton estate on behalf of the National Trust, which took over its ownership in 1946. The Throckmortons were a leading Catholic family during the Tudor-Stuart period when Catholics were persecuted, and Coughton Court at one time contained a priest hole, one of the hiding places for priests that were built into many of the principal Catholic houses of England at that time. Coughton Court is famous for its association with the failed Gunpowder Plot of 1605. The plotters were a band of devout Roman Catholics who had trusted King James I to allow them freedom of worship. When he reneged on his promise they planned to blow up the House of Lords whilst King James was attending the state opening of Parliament, which they hoped would result in the king's death, together with that of his young heir and all his lords and bishops.

THE GUNPOWDER PLOTTERS OF 1605 F6115

The conspirators then planned to kidnap King James's nine-year-old daughter Princess Elizabeth from her home at Coombe Abbey, near Coventry, have her crowned as a puppet queen and rule through her, eventually marrying her to a Catholic nobleman. Two of the main plotters – Francis Tresham and Robert Catesby – were grandsons of Sir Robert Throckmorton of Coughton Court (1513-1581), and although the Throckmorton of the day, Sir Thomas Throckmorton, prudently absented himself abroad, he allowed one of the conspirators, Sir Everard Digby, to use the house as a refuge and rallying point, from where he would mastermind the abduction of Princess Elizabeth. Lady Digby, her family and other women related to the plotters gathered in a room of the 16th-century gatehouse at Coughton Court on the night of 5th November to await news of the outcome of the affair. Also waiting with them were the Jesuit priest Father Henry Garnet, who had advised against the conspiracy all along and tried to prevent it, and Nicholas Owen, the famous priest-hole builder. However, when Robert Catesby's servant Thomas Bates galloped to Coughton in the early hours of November 6th 1605, leapt off his horse and ran into the gatehouse, he brought terrible news for them – Guy Fawkes has been apprehended in the cellars beneath the House of Lords on the point of lighting the fuse for the powder kegs, the plot had been discovered and foiled, and the conspirators were fleeing for their lives. Eventually all the Gunpowder Plotters were either killed during capture or apprehended and executed most horribly, as was the unfortunate Father Garnet. Nicholas Owen was also captured, and died under torture in the Tower of London, whilst being questioned.

Although the carriageway through its centre into the courtyard was later converted into an entrance hall, Coughton Court's beautiful gatehouse is still intact and you can see the place much as those people knew it in those turbulent times over 400 years ago – and some people visiting Coughton Court have reported hearing the sound of running footsteps near the gatehouse, perhaps a ghostly echo of Thomas Bates arriving with his news of disaster…

Studley is on the western edge of Warwickshire, near Redditch. Although this imposing building is known as Studley Castle, it is actually a country house constructed in the 1830s. Over the years it has housed a horticultural college and been used as offices for British Leyland and Rover Cars, but it is now the Studley Castle Hotel. According to Meg Elizabeth Atkins in her book 'Haunted Warwickshire' of 1981, Studley Castle is haunted by a Grey Lady who is sometimes heard sobbing or seen standing by a window on the first floor, sadly gazing out. Her name in her earthly life is not known, but the tale goes that her husband accused her of infidelity and in his jealous rage he snatched their young child from her arms and threw it to its death from the main tower. Distraught with grief, the lady rushed from the house and drowned herself in a nearby lake, and her unhappy shade has roamed the castle ever since. However, Rupert Matthews tells a similar story in his book 'Haunted Places of Warwickshire' of 2005, and although he also locates it in Studley, he says the house where the crime took place was demolished long ago, and that the lady's weeping and wailing spectre haunts the fields around the village, dressed in a long white dress – so who knows!

STUDLEY
STUDLEY CASTLE
c1960 S299017d

HENLEY-IN-ARDEN, THE WHITE SWAN HOTEL c1960 H414033

East of Studley is Henley-in-Arden, a pretty town sited at a crossroads between the A3400 and the A4189 roads west of Warwick. The town is noted for its long High Street lined with historic buildings in a variety of architectural styles. This photograph shows the White Swan Hotel in the High Street; the present building dates from c1600, but there is believed to have been an inn on this site since the 1350s. In the heyday of the stage coach it was a favourite stopping point on the road between Birmingham and London. Like many ancient inns, the White Swan is reputed to be haunted – the resident spectre here is the ghost of a young lady of dubious virtue called Virginia Black, who died after falling down the stairs following a quarrel with one of her clients in 1845; her shade is said to roam the corridor outside bedroom 17, but it has been some time now since she was last seen.

For many centuries Warwick has been dominated by its magnificent castle overlooking the River Avon, the ancient seat of the Earls of Warwick. An old ghost tale about Warwick Castle is that it used to be haunted by a spectral black dog with glowing red eyes that terrified everyone who saw it. It was widely believed that the phantom hound was the transmogrified spirit of Moll Bloxham, a resident of Warwick in the Middle Ages who stole milk and butter from the castle to sell from her cottage outside the castle walls. The Earl of Warwick of the time was so enraged when her theft was discovered that he ordered her to be publicly punished, but the sentence was enacted so severely that Moll pronounced a curse on the castle. She then disappeared, and soon afterwards the ghostly black dog with glowing red eyes began to be seen roaming around the castle grounds at night, and was widely believed to be an incarnation of Moll's vengeful spirit. Sightings of the dog were believed to be omens of doom. Eventually three clergymen were summoned to exorcise the creature. They drove the spectral dog to the top of Caesar's Tower in the castle, from where it jumped into the river below and was never seen again.

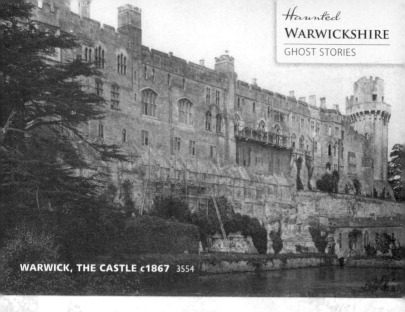

WARWICK, THE CASTLE c1867 3554

Several ghost stories are associated with Warwick Castle, but it is most famously haunted by the shade of a former owner, Sir Fulke Greville, 1st Baron Brooke (1554-1628). He was given the castle by King James I in 1612 and spent a huge amount of money restoring and beautifying it. In 1682 Sir Fulke Greville was attacked in London by his servant, Ralph Heywood, during an argument over what he was leaving Heywood in his will. Heywood stabbed him with his dagger, then, in horror at what he had done, killed himself by cutting his own throat. Sir Fulke Greville then suffered a lingering death from his infected wound. His body was brought back to Warwick and interred in the Collegiate Church of St Mary at the town. However, his spirit seems loathe to leave his former home that he loved so dearly – his ghost is said to materialise as a cloud of mist in the rooms he occupied in the Watergate Tower, now known as the Ghost Tower, and his pale, pain-wracked wraith is also supposed to emerge from his portrait in the castle on occasions and roam around the grounds, groaning in agony.

WARWICK, WESTGATE AND THE LORD LEYCESTER HOSPITAL 1892
31022

One of the most picturesque buildings in Warwick is The Lord Leycester Hospital at the top of the High Street adjoining the Westgate, one of the entrances into the medieval walled town. It was originally the Guild House of St George and the Blessed Virgin. In 1571 Robert Dudley, Earl of Leicester, acquired the buildings from the town burgesses and transformed them into a 'hospital' (almshouse) for 12 old disabled 'brethren' – usually ex-servicemen – and the Hospital still serves this function. For many years a headless ghost was said to wander through the rooms and passages of The Lord Leycester Hospital, but no one knew whose wraith he was, or why he walked there. Then a gruesome discovery was made at the Westgate, which perhaps explains the haunting – during renovations to the chapel of St James that stands over the Westgate, the headless body of a man dressed in a rusty suit of armour was discovered concealed in a blocked-up wall cavity. We shall never know now what terrible event took place there many years ago, but his remains were given proper burial and the spirit of the headless man seems now to rest in peace.

Someone who made quite an impact on Warwick in the past was Thomas Oken, a wealthy merchant and burgess of the town who died childless in 1573. He set up a charity providing almshouses, which continues to operate, and also left instructions for an annual feast to be held in his name, called Oken's Feast, which still takes place at the end of January each year at The Lord Leycester Hospital. Thomas Oken's former home, a quaint timber-framed house in Castle Street, is now the Thomas Oken Tea Rooms. Some people say that his spirit still occupies his old home, and his ghostly footsteps can sometimes be heard climbing the stairs.

Another place in Warwick that may be haunted is the Warwick Arms Hotel in the High Street, where some guests have reported seeing a mysterious 'faceless woman' in one of the bedrooms, who just faded away before their eyes when they tried to speak to her…

WARWICK, HIGH STREET AND THE WARWICK ARMS HOTEL 1922 72343

The legend of the medieval hero Guy of Warwick tells how he spent many years killing dangerous animals and men to prove his love for Felice, daughter of the Earl of Warwick. Eventually he married Felice and became Earl of Warwick on the death of her father, but not long after the wedding he went on a pilgrimage to the Holy Land. On his return to Warwick, full of remorse for all the deaths he had caused, he decided to live a secret and penitent life as a hermit in a cave above the River Avon, close to what is now the ruined Guy's Cliffe House at Warwick, unbeknown to Felice. She finally found him as he lay gravely ill, and nursed him until his death; only then did she realise who he was. Unable to live without him, she too died. One version of the tale says she threw herself in the river and drowned, whilst another says she pined away with a broken heart. Either way, her distraught ghost is said to have haunted the area around Guy's Cliffe House ever since.

WARWICK, GUY'S CLIFFE HOUSE FROM THE RIVER 1892 31036

Not far from Guy's Cliffe is Blacklow Hill, between Leek Wootton and Warwick. Standing in woodland on the hill adjacent to the A46, on the west side of the road just south of the junction with the A429, is Gaveston's Cross, a monument erected in 1821 to mark the point where Piers Gaveston, 1st Earl of Cornwall, was executed in 1312. The inscription on the monument is hard to decipher now, but reads: 'In the Hollow of this Rock, Was beheaded, On the 1st Day of July, 1312, By Barons lawless as himself, PIERS GAVESTON, Earl of Cornwall; The Minion of a hateful King: In Life and Death, A memorable Instance of Misrule.'

Gaveston was a Gascon knight who was the favourite, and probably the lover, of King Edward II. He encouraged the king in his despotic activities and was highly unpopular with the English barons because of his influence over him. He was particularly hated by the Earl of Warwick, whom Gaveston had offended by nicknaming him 'The Black Dog of Arden' because of his shaggy black hair. In 1312 the Earl of Lancaster and other noblemen declared war on the king, angered by his dependence on Gaveston rather than experienced lords. Gaveston was charged by the king to defend Scarborough Castle and did so with great courage until his food supplies ran out and he was forced to yield. He was then promised safe conduct to London and taken as far as Oxfordshire, but when the Earl of Warwick heard about Gaveston's whereabouts he rode out with a force of men-at-arms to capture him. The Earl took Gaveston back to Warwick Castle, and at dawn the following morning he was tied to a horse mockingly bedecked with ribbons and jingling bells. A cavalcade of armed men then took him to Blacklow Hill, where he was beheaded, a summary execution that shocked many people even in those brutal times. There is a local legend that a ghostly re-enactment of the procession taking Gaveston to the scene of his murder can sometimes be seen ascending the hill, accompanied by the eerie sound of the tinkling bells worn by his horse.

KENILWORTH, ST NICHOLAS'S CHURCH 1892 30946

The parish church of St Nicholas at Kenilworth was built c1190 and later remodelled in the Perpendicular style, but it was heavily 'restored' in the 19th century. It stands at the north-east corner of Abbey Fields, so called because this was once the site of Kenilworth's Abbey of St Mary the Virgin; this was a community of Augustinian canons (known as Black Canons, because of the black habits they wore) that was founded as a priory in the 12th century and became so wealthy and powerful that it was raised to abbey status in 1447. In the 1530s King Henry VIII dissolved the monasteries and St Mary's Abbey was signed over the Crown. Most of the buildings were dismantled, and their stone re-used elsewhere. However, some traces remain, both in the open spaces of Abbey Fields and within the churchyard around St Nicholas's Church. The photograph on the opposite page shows the remains of the gatehouse in the churchyard, built between 1361 and 1375, which was formerly the main entrance to the abbey.

The former abbey site at Kenilworth was comprehensively excavated in the 1880s when the ruins of the old abbey church and cloisters were discovered; it was decided to leave the ruins exposed, and they now form part of the churchyard of St Nicholas. However, it seems that ghostly monks, or more correctly Black Canons, roam the area where they lived and worshipped in their earthly lives. Over the years a number of people have heard what seems to be the faint sound of monastic chanting and choral responses coming from the area around the ruined church, disembodied voices that seem to be an echo from the past. For many centuries there has also been a local tradition that a procession of ghostly monks sometimes glides along the path between the avenue of trees leading from the west door of the church of St Nicholas towards Abbey Fields, their cowled heads bowed in silent prayer. For many years the phantom procession just seemed to vanish away at a certain point – then when the 19th-century excavations revealed the ruins of the old abbey church, its main entrance was found to be exactly at the point where the spectral monks always disappeared…

KENILWORTH, THE OLD PRIORY GATEWAY IN THE CHURCHYARD 1892 30947

The first stone castle at Kenilworth was built in the 1120s, and the main keep was constructed in 1162. In 1563 Queen Elizabeth I gave the castle to Robert Dudley, Earl of Leicester, who lavished huge sums of money turning it into a magnificent private house fit to receive the queen, who he famously entertained there for 19 days in 1575. The castle changed hands several times during the Civil War, after which it was 'slighted' by order of Parliament to prevent it being of further military use. The north side of the keep was blown up, breaches were blasted in the outer walls, and the Great Mere, or lake, that formed part of its defences was drained. A ghostly monk is said to roam the grounds of the castle, and there is also an old tale that a phantom coach drawn by four spectral horses drives out of the old southern gateway, thunders over the embankment that was once a causeway over the Great Mere and then heads off at high speed towards the former King's Arms and Castle Hotel at the corner of The Square and Station Road in Kenilworth – however, this apparition only appears once every hundred years!

KENILWORTH CASTLE IN THE DAYS OF QUEEN ELIZABETH I K5303

KENILWORTH, THE GATEHOUSE c1955 K5004

The Gatehouse at Kenilworth was constructed by Robert Dudley, Earl of Leicester as part of his embellishments to the castle in the 16th century. Its top floor now houses an exhibition about Queen Elizabeth I and Robert Dudley. Also in this building is the Elizabethan Bedroom, which features an impressive 'Tester' bed dating from the 1590s. At the foot of the bed is a wooden baby's crib, which a former manager of the castle once discovered mysteriously rocking from side to side when no one else was in the room, as if being pushed by an unseen hand…

In the 1970s a local lady attending a function in the Gatehouse saw the ghost of a young woman materialise in a room on the first floor – but no one else saw her, even though the room was full of people. The witness saw the ghostly lady sitting in the deep bay of one of the windows as she worked on a piece of needlework, and was particularly struck by the air of quiet contentment that she felt emanating from the apparition. Whoever she is, the spectral lady who lingers in the Gatehouse seems to be a happy spirit.

A few miles west of Kenilworth is Baddesley Clinton, a medieval moated manor house that was the home of the Ferrers family for centuries; it is now in the care of the National Trust. Baddesley Clinton was a refuge for Catholic priests during the period of religious persecution of the 16th and 17th centuries, and has several priest holes from that time.

There are many eerie tales about this atmospheric building. The sound of men's voices raised in argument has been heard coming from empty rooms, objects have been found in mysterious disarray in rooms left tidy when last used, and disembodied footsteps have been heard by many people coming along the corridor on the Upper Landing of the house, sometimes in daylight but most often at night. Some people have reported hearing the footsteps coming along the corridor and stopping outside their bedroom, and then seeing the handle of the door to their room being turned, although when they open the door the corridor is empty. One person this happened to was the artist Rebecca Ferrers (née Orpen), who lived at Baddesley Clinton from 1867 when she married Marmion Ferrers until her death in 1923; many of her paintings are displayed in the house, including her self-portrait which was painted in 1885, the year of her second marriage to Edward Dering after Marmion Ferrers died. Rebecca recorded the unnerving experience of hearing 'that solemn tread' in her diary: 'It had an indescribably awful and mournful sound…and affected me deeply…It had a very weird effect to hear the handle jerked loudly within a few feet of where you are standing, and see no-one.'

Another restless spirit of the house is a fair-haired lady dressed in a dark gown – a guest staying there in the 1880s saw the apparition gliding past her bed in the Tapestry Bedroom before it vanished through the door, but the ghostly lady has also been seen in other bedrooms and upper floor corridors. She is thought to be the shade of a Lady Ferrers who lived there in the mid 17th century, but no one knows why her spectre wanders her former home.

Baddesley Clinton passed to the Ferrers family through the marriage of the daughter and heiress of a previous owner, Nicholas Brome, to Sir Edward Ferrers in 1517. Nicholas Brome is a notorious character in the house's history, a hot-tempered man who committed two murders and got away with it. His father had bought the manor of Baddesley Clinton in 1438 but fell into a dispute with John Herthill, the Steward of the Duke of Warwick, which culminated with Herthill murdering him in 1468. Three years later Nicholas Brome avenged his father's murder when he attacked Herthill so violently that he died of his injuries. He was ordered to do penance for his crime and pay compensation to Herthill's widow, but suffered no further punishment. Having inherited Baddesley Clinton in 1483, Nicholas Brome got more blood on his hands in 1485 when he returned home to find his wife in the parlour cuddled up with a man tickling her under the chin. Assuming they were having an affair, Nicholas drew his sword and slew the man on the spot, before realising he had killed the parish priest who was merely giving his wife some words of comfort. Nicholas again managed to buy his way out of retribution and was granted a pardon for the crime by both King Henry VII and the Pope, but the Pope ordered him to atone for his deed by erecting towers on St Michael's Church at Baddesley Clinton and St Giles Church at Packwood, a few miles away – these are known locally as the Towers of Atonement. Nicholas Brome died on 10th October 1517, full of contrition for his crimes. He was buried just outside the south door of the church at Baddesley Clinton, as he directed in his will, so 'people may tread upon mee when they come into church'. Perhaps his ghost or that of the priest he murdered is one of the spirits that haunts Baddesley Clinton house – or perhaps they both do – but every ten years, on the anniversary of his death, Nicholas Brome's wraith is said to walk from the house up the path to the doorway of the church, where it disappears at the spot where his remains lie interred.

LEAMINGTON SPA, ROYAL PUMP ROOM AND THE PARISH CHURCH 1922 72442

Leamington Spa developed from a small village into one of the most fashionable watering places in 19th-century England after William Abbotts discovered a mineral spring on land in what is now Bath Street in the 1790s, and established the original baths. Soon more springs were discovered and developed, and large numbers of visitors came to Leamington Spa to 'take the waters'. The legacy of the Leamington's heyday as a place of fashion and prosperity still remains in the grand Georgian and early Victorian architecture of many parts of the vibrant modern town of today. As part of the facilities for the spa resort, the Upper Assembly Rooms building on the corner of the Parade and Regent Street was erected in 1812, which held balls, concerts and public meetings with facilities for playing cards, billiards or just reading. In 1887 the building was taken over by P H Woodward's, 'silk mercers and drapers', which became one of Leamington's long-lasting businesses; it is seen in that role in the 1950s in the photograph on the opposite page, where it is the second building from the left.

The Woodward's department store in Leamington Spa closed in 2004 and its former site has now been redeveloped as contemporary luxury apartments, but although the main building was demolished, its original façade from the first floor level was retained, with a new building constructed behind it. The old Woodward's premises was said to be the site of several mysterious occurrences. A ghost of a woman known as Annie was believed to roam the top floor of the building, and the sound of a child screaming and crying was once heard, coming from a cupboard in the basement of the store. When shop staff traced the sound and looked inside the cupboard, it was found to be empty. Staff also believed that the store was the scene of poltergeist activity after items in the soft furnishings department were found thrown in disarray around the shop floor one Monday morning, after being left tidy before the store was closed on the preceding Saturday evening. There was no evidence of a break-in or theft. It remains to be seen whether the unquiet spirits that roamed the old Woodward's building will return to haunt the new building that now stands on the site…

LEAMINGTON SPA, THE PARADE c1955 L25047D

SOUTHAM, THE MANOR HOUSE AND MARKET HILL c1960 S298030

About seven miles east of Leamington Spa is Southam. This is predominately a dormitory town now, but it is a historic place. Roman coins have been found in the churchyard, and a market charter was granted by Henry III in 1227. Southam stands astride the Welsh Road used by cattle drovers in the past, and in the early 19th century it was a stop for coaches such as the London-Warwick-Birmingham Mail, the Express and the Sovereign. King Charles I lodged in the town before the Civil War battle of Edghill in 1642, staying in the town's old manor house on Market Hill that is now partly occupied by Southam Pharmacy – the gabled corner building seen on the left of this view as it looked when it was photographed c1960, before the timber-framing on its exterior was exposed, as it appears today. The king imposed a heavy fine on the town when he arrived, as Southam's Rector supported Parliament and failed to ring the church bells to welcome him to the town.

According to local tradition, the 14th-century building in Coventry Street in Southam known as The Old Mint (now a pub) is so named because King Charles I came back to the town following the battle of Edghill and demanded that the local gentry bring him their silverware to be melted down there and minted into coins so he could pay his army. Both the Old Mint and the old manor house building on Market Hill are said to be haunted. The ghost that roams the old manor is possibly the unquiet spirit of a servant from some long forgotten time, whose spectral footsteps are sometimes heard on walking along a corridor on the floor above the Southam Pharmacy shop; they have also been heard on the staircase of the Rockingham's cycles and motorcycles shop that adjoins the Pharmacy on the right hand side of the building – the part of the building with the large window seen to its right in the 1960's view on the opposite page, when it was being used as part of the Central Garage.

SOUTHAM, THE OLD MINT c1960 S298038

A short distance north of Southam, the Blue Lias Inn is located beside the Grand Union Canal on Stockton Road, a minor road linking the A423 and the A426 between the villages of Long Itchington and Stockton. The building was an 18th-century farmhouse before it became a canalside hostelry, and is said to be haunted by the red-haired ghost of a handsome farm labourer who caught the eye of the farmer's wife. One day the farmer returned home from market to find the couple in bed together; a violent scene ensued, which ended when the enraged husband killed the farmhand in front of his faithless wife. The wraith of the murdered man is supposed to haunt that upstairs room of the inn where he met his end, which is notable for having a strange, uncanny atmosphere and always being cold, despite the temperature elsewhere in the building. The shade of a one-legged farmer who lived in the inn building in the late 1700s is also said to linger in the room and is supposed to be responsible for the distinctive sound of uneven footsteps that some people have heard there at night, one being the heavy tread of his good leg and the other being the lighter tap of his wooden peg-leg on the floorboards.

East of Southam is Napton-on-the-Hill, Warwickshire's only true hilltop village. Napton's medieval church of St Lawrence is sited on the top of the hill above the village, in an isolated position some distance from the nearest houses. The ghostly forms of two ladies are said to haunt the church, dressed in grey gowns of 16th-century fashion. They manifest in the front pew, where they kneel as if deep in prayer. Sometimes there are no sightings of them for years, and then they might appear for several days running. No one knows whose quiet spirits they are, but these ghostly parishioners from the past obviously loved this ancient place of worship in their earthly life and are unwilling to leave it.

Another pub in this part of Warwickshire that is reputed to be haunted is the Plough Inn at Eathorpe, east of Leamington Spa. The Plough stands beside the B4455 road that runs diagonally across the county on the route of the Fosse Way, the Roman road that linked Exeter with Lincoln. The spirit of a traveller or former resident of the inn from the past still seems to linger there, for a strange shadowy figure has been seen walking across the bar area. Perhaps this ghost has a playful side, for on one occasion a member of staff at the pub distinctly felt the sensation of being prodded on the shoulder with a playful finger whilst mopping the floor – but no one else was nearby…

North of Eathorpe is Princethorpe, where an area of woodland to the west of the village is so famous for the ghostly nun reputed to walk there that it is called Nun Wood. A witness who saw the spectral nun in the 1950s recounted how she was dressed in a brown habit, and walked soundlessly through the wood towards him; as she got nearer, she seemed completely unaware of his presence – and then passed straight through him as she went on her way. When he had regained his composure and turned round to see where she was going, she had disappeared.

North of Princethorpe, the A45 road runs south of Rugby to Coventry. A stretch of this road around Knightlow Hill near Ryton-on-Dunsmore is said to be haunted by a phantom lorry that appears sometimes on foggy winter nights and careers along the wrong side of the road as if out of control. Over the years a number of motorists driving along the road have reported seeing the spectral lorry, which suddenly loomed out of the fog, headlights blazing, and seemed to be heading straight for them, forcing them to swerve their cars to the side of the road to avoid it – then, just at the last minute, the lorry vanished away as if it was never there at all…

WARWICKSHIRE

GHOST STORIES

One of Warwickshire's most famous ghost stories is the tale of 'One Handed Boughton'. In his earthly life, in the 16th century, Squire Boughton lived at Little Lawford Hall, close to the village of Long Lawford a short distance west of Rugby. He was a colourful and notorious character who acquired his land through fair and foul means and then zealously guarded his property; it was his custom to travel around his estate in a horse-drawn coach checking that all was well, and although the most common explanation for his nickname is that he lost a hand in an accident, the oldest account of his story is that he had it chopped off as the punishment meted out to him when he was taken to court for moving the boundary markers of his estate during a dispute with a neighbour.

After his death One Handed Boughton's ghost continued to drive around the Little Lawford area at night in a phantom coach drawn by six black horses, accompanied by the sound of thundering hooves and the crack of his whip as he urged them on; his apparition scared the local people so much that they were afraid to go out at night for fear of meeting him. His ghost also lingered in the bedroom of his former home, terrifying all who slept there to such an extent that the room had to be shut up and no longer used. Then in the mid 18th century Sir Edward Boughton decided to put an end to his ghostly ancestor's activities, and summoned twelve clergymen to Little Lawford Hall to perform an exorcism. They did this in the haunted bedroom, each holding a lighted candle as they performed the ceremony, but one by one the candles went out, until only one was left alight as the clergymen struggled to lay the ghost of One Handed Boughton.

In the darkness of the room, lit by the feeble glow of that one candle, the clergymen eventually succeeded in confining One Handed Boughton's spirit into a glass bottle which was firmly sealed and stoppered-up and then thrown into a pool in the grounds. The bottle remained undisturbed in the pond for many years, but in the 1880s it was retrieved by a young boy who was fishing there. By this time Squire Boughton's former home of Little Lawford Hall had been demolished and his family descendants were living at their new home of Brownsover Hall, just north of Rugby, so the bottle was taken there for the family to keep safe. One Handed Boughton's spirit seemed to be reactivated as soon as the bottle arrived at Brownsover Hall, and he lost no time in haunting the new family home in all his old ways, even though the bottle was kept secure in a locked cupboard – on many occasions the door to the room where it was kept was seen opening and closing of its own accord! The sound of footsteps, groans and voices was heard coming from empty rooms and corridors of Brownsover Hall, especially from the tower, as well as the clattering of ghostly hooves and crunch of wheels on the drive outside the house, as One Handed Boughton drove his phantom coach around the grounds…and although the Ward-Boughton-Leigh family had the bottle buried and encased in concrete in a secret location when they left Brownsover Hall after the Second World War, some people say that his ghost has not been laid to rest and continues to haunt the house, which is now the Brownsover Hall Hotel.

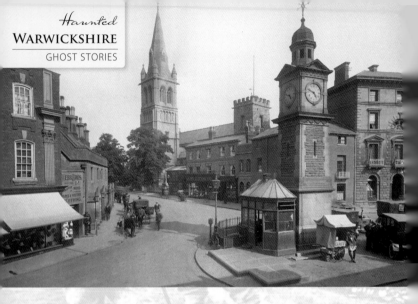

RUGBY, THE CLOCK TOWER AND ST ANDREW'S CHURCH 1922
72125

The busy market town of Rugby is the second largest town in
Warwickshire. It gained its market charter in 1255, with its medieval
market place situated at the intersection of ancient roadways
linking Leicester to Oxford and Northampton to Coventry. Rugby
celebrated Queen Victoria's Golden Jubilee in 1887 with the erection
of the Jubilee Clock Tower in the market place, which still stands
majestically in the town today.

Theatres are notoriously haunted places, and the Rugby Theatre
in Henry Street is no exception – the stalls of the auditorium are
reputed to be roamed by the spectre of a man who fell to his death
from the balcony above, whilst the area backstage is roamed by the
ghost of an old actor who died peacefully at home of old age, but
whose spirit has chosen to linger in the building that he loved so well
in his earthly life.

A few miles to the east of Coventry is Coombe Country Park, a public recreational area that was developed from the grounds of Coombe Abbey, a Cistercian monastery founded in the 12th century. The abbey was closed in 1539 and its buildings were converted into a private house which has been much extended and altered over the years into the magnificent mansion that stands today, now the Coombe Abbey Hotel. The cowled figure of a ghostly monk is said to glide around the grounds of Coombe Abbey. No one knows who he is, but he may be the wraith of Abbot Geoffrey who was brutally murdered at the abbey in 1345. Records show that King Edward III ordered an inquiry into his murder, but the account of its findings has been lost – so we will never know the reason for the crime, or who committed it. Perhaps the murderer was never found and punished for his deed, and that is why the ghost of the unfortunate Abbot Geoffrey cannot rest.

A sad love story is linked with the graveyard of the Church of St John the Baptist at Wolvey in north Warwickshire, south-east of Nuneaton. Many years ago a group of gypsies camped near Wolvey, and one of the gypsy girls fell deeply in love with a young man from the village, as he did with her. The girl chose to follow her heart and gave up the travelling life to marry the young man and settle in the village. The couple were blissfully happy together, but the following summer the girl died in childbirth, and her baby with her. Her grief-stricken husband visited their grave every day for the next year, then on the anniversary of their deaths his body was found lying beside it – he had died of a broken heart. He was buried in the grave beside his wife and child. The ghosts of the lovers are said to appear in the churchyard every July, united once again as they walk along together, the young wife lovingly cradling her baby in her arms.

Nuneaton derives its name from a priory for nuns that was founded there in 1150, and developed into a busy market town in the Middle Ages. The construction of the Coventry Canal in the late 18th century, and the fact that the coalfield town of Nuneaton later became a busy railway junction, made the town a busy manufacturing centre from the early 19th century onwards. There were coal mines, brick and tile manufacturers, iron works, worsted factories, cotton and silk goods manufacturers and ribbon makers to be found here. The Albion Buildings (or Albion Works) in Attleborough Road were originally a row of three-storeyed silk weavers cottages, with ribbon weavers' looms on the upper storey. The Albion Buildings are now used for commercial purposes and are said to be haunted by the harmless but mischievous ghost of an old lady who turns electric lights on and off and tampers with the office equipment. This playful ghost is presumed to be the shade of a silk weaver who lived or worked here in her earthly life.

Many of Nuneaton's old buildings were swept away during redevelopment of the town and road construction in the second half of the 20th century, but one that still survives is the former Bulls Head Inn at 25 Abbey Street (later called The Courtyard), which now houses the India Red restaurant – the building with the three points on its roof frontage in the centre distance of the view on the opposite page, on the right-hand side of the road just past the block of white painted buildings. In the days when this was an inn, a landlord once saw the ghostly figure of an old lady in the bar one night when he was locking up. He described the spectral lady as wearing old-fashioned clothes in the style of a Victorian grandmother. He wondered who she was and what she was doing there, then after a few seconds she left the building – by walking out through a solid wall.

NUNEATON, ABBEY STREET c1960 N89038

Another ghostly lady dressed in black clothing of 19th-century fashion, and with her face covered with a veil, is reputed to haunt the Griffin Inn near Bedworth, which is sited beside the B4113 (Coventry Road) just off the Griff roundabout south of Nuneaton. Her restless spirit has been active there for many years and has been seen by several licensees of the pub over the years, usually manifesting in their bedrooms during the night. She is also supposed to be responsible for the mysterious sound of knocking and tapping that comes from the cellar and for tampering with the compressed air cylinders and beer taps, which are sometimes found inexplicably turned off. This ghost also seems to have developed a gambling streak over the years – on one occasion, the landlady was standing alone in the bar when the one-armed bandit machine suddenly came to life and spewed out £70 in tokens as its invisible player won the jackpot – but it was switched off at the mains at the time…

South-west of Nuneaton is the ruined shell of Astley Castle, a fortified 16th-century manor house that was ravaged by fire in 1978. In the 16th century this was the childhood home of Lady Jane Grey, the tragic teenage girl known to history as 'The Nine Days Queen'. Of royal descent, she was set up as a puppet queen by her father-in-law, the Duke of Northumberland, as a Protestant claimant to the throne after the death of King Henry VIII's son and successor King Edward VI in 1553 in preference to the Roman Catholic Princess Mary, King Henry's daughter by his first queen, Katharine of Aragon. Jane ruled for nine days before Mary raised an army, overthrew the coup and took her rightful place on the throne as Queen Mary I. Lady Jane was then imprisoned in the Tower of London before being beheaded in 1554. Her ghost is said to have returned home to Warwickshire where it haunts the grounds of Astley Castle. Some witnesses have described seeing her spectre sitting in the grounds quietly reading a book, as this devout and intellectual young girl so often did in life, so her ghost has obviously kept its head – unlike the wraith of her father, Henry Grey, Duke of Suffolk, which also roams Astley Castle. His phantom is headless, as he was beheaded in 1554 for taking part in the Wyatt rebellion against Queen Mary. After the failure of the uprising Henry Grey fled home to Astley, where he hid for several days in a hollow oak tree near the castle. Eventually he was betrayed by the servant who was helping him and was taken to London to meet the executioner's axe.

Another ruined Tudor mansion stands to the west of Nuneaton at Hartshill, known as Hartshill Castle because its crumbling remains stand on the earthworks of an early castle that was built here. A ghostly lady dressed in a long black gown of Elizabethan fashion is supposed to haunt the ruins – if you see her and she just passes you by, then all will be well, but bad luck will come to you if she seems aware of your presence and glances at you as she walks past!

POLESWORTH, THE GATEHOUSE 1924 76124

In the northern tip of Warwickshire is Polesworth, where an abbey was founded by King Egbert in AD827, who installed his daughter Editha as its first abbess. Now serving as the village's parish church, the Abbey Church of St Editha in Polesworth dates from Norman times, and contains an effigy of an abbess dating from c1200; this is too late to represent Editha, but is believed to be the earliest effigy of an abbess in England. The abbey's 14th-century gatehouse is seen in this view. Together with the oldest parts of the church, it is all that now remains of Polesworth Abbey. The abbey was closed down by King Henry VIII and the property passed to Francis Goodere in 1544, who dismantled most of its buildings to provide stone for his new manor house, Polesworth Hall, which was itself demolished in the 19th century. The story goes that the ghost of St Edith appeared in the abbey whilst the buildings were being demolished, frightening the workmen to such an extent that they downed tools for a while – but in the end her spectre was powerless to prevent the destruction of her beloved abbey, and now her sad ghost wanders between the abbey church and the gatehouse.

FRANCIS FRITH

PIONEER   VICTORIAN   PHOTOGRAPHER

Francis Frith, founder of the world-famous photographic archive, was a complex and multi-talented man. A devout Quaker and a highly successful Victorian businessman, he was philosophical by nature and pioneering in outlook. By 1855 he had already established a wholesale grocery business in Liverpool, and sold it for the astonishing sum of £200,000, which is the equivalent today of over £15,000,000. Now in his thirties, and captivated by the new science of photography, Frith set out on a series of pioneering journeys up the Nile and to the Near East.

INTRIGUE AND EXPLORATION

He was the first photographer to venture beyond the sixth cataract of the Nile. Africa was still the mysterious 'Dark Continent', and Stanley and Livingstone's historic meeting was a decade into the future. The conditions for picture taking confound belief. He laboured for hours in his wicker dark-room in the sweltering heat of the desert, while the volatile chemicals fizzed dangerously in their trays. Back in London he exhibited his photographs and was 'rapturously cheered' by members of the Royal Society. His reputation as a photographer was made overnight.

VENTURE OF A LIFE-TIME

By the 1870s the railways had threaded their way across the country, and Bank Holidays and half-day Saturdays had been made obligatory by Act of Parliament. All of a sudden the working man and his family were able to enjoy days out, take holidays, and see a little more of the world.

With typical business acumen, Francis Frith foresaw that these new tourists would enjoy having souvenirs to commemorate their days out. For the next thirty years he travelled the country by train and by pony and trap, producing fine photographs of seaside resorts and beauty spots that were keenly bought by millions of Victorians. These prints were painstakingly pasted into family albums and pored over during the dark nights of winter, rekindling precious memories of summer excursions. Frith's studio was soon supplying retail shops all over the country, and by 1890 F Frith & Co had become the greatest specialist photographic publishing company in the world, with over 2,000 sales outlets, and pioneered the picture postcard.

FRANCIS FRITH'S LEGACY

Francis Frith had died in 1898 at his villa in Cannes, his great project still growing. By 1970 the archive he created contained over a third of a million pictures showing 7,000 British towns and villages.

Frith's legacy to us today is of immense significance and value, for the magnificent archive of evocative photographs he created provides a unique record of change in the cities, towns and villages throughout Britain over a century and more. Frith and his fellow studio photographers revisited locations many times down the years to update their views, compiling for us an enthralling and colourful pageant of British life and character.

We are fortunate that Frith was dedicated to recording the minutiae of everyday life. For it is this sheer wealth of visual data, the painstaking chronicle of changes in dress, transport, street layouts, buildings, housing and landscape that captivates us so much today, offering us a powerful link with the past and with the lives of our ancestors.

Computers have now made it possible for Frith's many thousands of images to be accessed almost instantly. The archive offers every one of us an opportunity to examine the places where we and our families have lived and worked down the years. Its images, depicting our shared past, are now bringing pleasure and enlightenment to millions around the world a century and more after his death.

For further information visit: www.francisfrith.com

INTERIOR DECORATION

Frith's photographs can be seen framed and as giant wall murals in thousands of pubs, restaurants, hotels, banks, retail stores and other public buildings throughout Britain. These provide interesting and attractive décor, generating strong local interest and acting as a powerful reminder of gentler days in our increasingly busy and frenetic world.

FRITH PRODUCTS

All Frith photographs are available as prints and posters in a variety of different sizes and styles. In the UK we also offer a range of other gift and stationery products illustrated with Frith photographs, although many of these are not available for delivery outside the UK – see our web site for more information on the products available for delivery in your country.

THE INTERNET

Over 100,000 photographs of Britain can be viewed and purchased on the Frith web site. The web site also includes memories and reminiscences contributed by our customers, who have personal knowledge of localities and of the people and properties depicted in Frith photographs. If you wish to learn more about a specific town or village you may find these reminiscences fascinating to browse. Why not add your own comments if you think they would be of interest to others? See **www.francisfrith.com**

PLEASE HELP US BRING FRITH'S PHOTOGRAPHS TO LIFE

Our authors do their best to recount the history of the places they write about. They give insights into how particular towns and villages developed, they describe the architecture of streets and buildings, and they discuss the lives of famous people who lived there. But however knowledgeable our authors are, the story they tell is necessarily incomplete.

Frith's photographs are so much more than plain historical documents. They are living proofs of the flow of human life down the generations. They show real people at real moments in history; and each of those people is the son or daughter of someone, the brother or sister, aunt or uncle, grandfather or grandmother of someone else. All of them lived, worked and played in the streets depicted in Frith's photographs.

We would be grateful if you would give us your insights into the places shown in our photographs: the streets and buildings, the shops, businesses and industries. Post your memories of life in those streets on the Frith website: what it was like growing up there, who ran the local shop and what shopping was like years ago; if your workplace is shown tell us about your working day and what the building is used for now. Read other visitors' memories and reconnect with your shared local history and heritage. With your help more and more Frith photographs can be brought to life, and vital memories preserved for posterity, and for the benefit of historians in the future.

Wherever possible, we will try to include some of your comments in future editions of our books. Moreover, if you spot errors in dates, titles or other facts, please let us know, because our archive records are not always completely accurate—they rely on 140 years of human endeavour and hand-compiled records. You can email us using the contact form on the website.

Thank you!

For further information, trade, or author enquiries
please contact us at the address below:

**The Francis Frith Collection, 6 Oakley Business Park,
Wylye Road, Dinton, Wiltshire SP3 5EU.**
Tel: +44 (0)1722 716 376 Fax: +44 (0)1722 716 881
e-mail: sales@francisfrith.co.uk **www.francisfrith.com**